The Essent

Waffle Cookbook

Try A Waffle for Breakfast, Lunch or Dinner

BY: SOPHIA FREEMAN

© 2019 Sophia Freeman All Rights Reserved

★ ★ ★ ★ ★ ★ ★ ★ ★ ★ ★

COPYRIGHTED

Liability

This publication is meant as an informational tool. The individual purchaser accepts all liability if damages occur because of following the directions or guidelines set out in this publication. The Author bears no responsibility for reparations caused by the misuse or misinterpretation of the content.

Copyright

The content of this publication is solely for entertainment purposes and is meant to be purchased by one individual. Permission is not given to any individual who copies, sells or distributes parts or the whole of this publication unless it is explicitly given by the Author in writing.

* * * * ★ ★ ★ ★ ★ * *

Table of Contents

Introduction 6

1. Waffles I 8
2. Whole-grain waffles 10
3. Classic waffles 13
4. Tender and Easy Buttermilk Waffles 15
5. Easy French Toast Waffles 17
6. Buttermilk Waffles 19
7. Waffles II 21
8. Whole Wheat Oat Waffles 24
9. Potato Waffles 27
10. Mom's Waffles 29
11. Chocolate Chip Waffles 31
12. Cornmeal waffles 34
13. Buttermilk Prairie Waffles 36

14. Chocolate Waffles I 38

15. Puff pastry waffles 41

16. Wonderful Waffles 43

17. Pumpkin Waffles 46

18. Belgian Waffles 50

19. Deluxe Waffles 52

20. Easy Waffles 54

21. Banana Waffles 57

22. Norwegian Waffles 59

23. Yeast Waffles 61

24. Blueberries Waffles 64

25. Cinnamon Pumpkin Waffles 67

26. Almond Flour waffles 70

27. Yogurt Waffles 72

28. Gingerbread Waffles with Hot Chocolate 74

29. Beer Batter Waffles 77

30. Vegan Waffles 79

Conclusion 82

About the Author 83

Author's Afterthoughts 85

Introduction

When my kids were little they would always ask me for waffles for breakfast. They would take the maple syrup out of the refrigerator and pour heaps of sugary sauce over a waffle heated up in the toaster. Those days of sugar-filled ready frozen waffles with no nutritional value are over! Now, when my family asks me to prepare a meal I use natural ingredients to make my batter and an excellent waffle iron.

It is always important to look at the manufacturer's specifications when using a waffle iron as one uses more batter than another. The different models can also cook the batter in different times, so give the manual a read before cooking. The recipes in this cookbook are easy to prepare and taste fresher than any frozen waffles found in the store.

1. Waffles I

These classic waffles are excellent for breakfast or brunch food. All you need are a few simple ingredients and a good waffle maker.

Preparation Time-5 minutes

Servings-6

Ingredients

- 2 large eggs, beaten
- 16 ounces all-purpose flour
- 14 ounces milk
- 4 ounces vegetable oil
- ½ ounce white sugar
- 2/3 ounce baking powder
- ½ teaspoon vanilla extract
- ¼ teaspoon salt

Directions

1. Preheat waffle maker according to manufacturer's instructions.

2. In a large mixing bowl, beat all **Ingredients** together until smooth.

3. Spray waffle iron with a cooking spray and pour the batter into the iron. Cook until both sides are evenly browned and serve.

2. Whole-Grain Waffles

These waffles make a healthy alternative to toast, eggs and bacon for breakfast. I like to eat these with some berries on the side and a hot cup of coffee.

Preparation Time-10 minutes

Servings-6

Ingredients

- 2 beaten eggs
- 14 ounces skim milk
- 2 ounces canola oil
- 2 ounces applesauce, unsweetened
- 1 teaspoon vanilla extract
- 8 ounces whole wheat pastry flour
- 4 ounces flax seed meal
- 2 ounces wheat germ
- 2 ounces all-purpose flour
- 2/3 ounce baking powder
- ½ ounce sugar
- ¼ teaspoon salt

Directions

1. Preheat waffle iron.

2. Beat eggs, skim milk, canola oil, applesauce and vanilla extract together in a large mixing bowl until combined.

3. Coat the waffle iron with a cooking spray and then pour batter in to the iron according to manufacturer's instructions. Cook until browned evenly on both sides and serve.

3. Classic Waffles

The traditional waffle recipe is always the best and reminds me of mealtime as a kid. My mother would cook up some of these waffles on weekends and serve them with butter and cream.

Preparation Time-10 minutes

Servings-5

Ingredients

- 16 ounces all-purpose flour
- 1 teaspoon salt
- 2/3 ounce baking powder
- 1 ounce white sugar
- 2 large eggs
- 12 ounces warm milk
- 2 ½ ounces melted butter
- 1 teaspoon vanilla extract

Directions

1. Preheat waffle iron

2. Combine flour, salt, baking powder and white sugar in a large mixing bowl and mix well.

3. Beat eggs in another mixing bowl and stir in warm milk, melted butter and vanilla extract.

4. Add wet mixture to dry and beat until smooth.

5. Pour batter into the waffle iron and cook until both sides are evenly browned.

4.Tender and Easy Buttermilk Waffles

These buttermilk waffles are tasty and filling. I like to serve these with some applesauce, sour cream and berries.

Preparation Time-15 minutes

Servings-6

Ingredients

- 16 ounces all-purpose flour
- 1 ounce white sugar
- 1/3 ounce baking powder
- 1 teaspoon baking soda
- ½ teaspoon salt
- 16 ounces low-fat buttermilk
- 2 ½ ounces butter, melted
- 2 lightly beaten eggs
- 1 teaspoon vanilla extract

Directions

1. Preheat waffle iron

2. Mix flour, white sugar, baking powder, soda and salt in a large mixing bowl until combined.

3. Beat eggs, buttermilk, butter and vanilla together. Stir wet mixture into dry until smooth and pour into the waffle iron. Cook until both sides are evenly browned and serve.

5. Easy French Toast Waffles

Why choose between French toast and waffles for breakfast when you can have both? I like to serve these with some cottage cheese and fresh berries on the side.

Preparation Time-15 minutes

Servings-2

Ingredients

- cooking spray
- 4 ounces whole milk
- 2 eggs
- ½ ounce maple syrup
- ½ teaspoon vanilla extract
- a pinch salt
- 4 pieces brioche, ½" thick

Directions

1. Preheat a waffle iron. Coat surface of iron lightly with a cooking spray.

2. Beat milk, eggs, syrup, vanilla and salt together in a large mixing bowl until well combined.

3. Dip brioche slices in mixture and place on a baking sheet with a rim to soak for 2 minutes.

4. Place soaked bread in the waffle iron and cook for 3-5 minutes until evenly browned.

6. Buttermilk Waffles

Buttermilk brings out a creamy and deliciously rich flavour in waffles that I love. Try these with some confectioners' sugar sprinkled on top and fresh strawberries.

Preparation Time-15 minutes

Servings-4

Ingredients

- 8 ounces all-purpose flour
- ½ ounce white sugar
- ¼ teaspoon salt
- ½ teaspoon baking soda
- 8 ounces buttermilk
- 1 egg
- ½ ounce vegetable oil

Directions

1. Preheat your waffle iron and then preheat oven to 275 degrees Fahrenheit. Place a baking rack on a cooking sheet and place in the oven.

2. In a big mixing bowl, whisk flour, white sugar, soda and salt together until well combined.

3. Beat the remaining wet **Ingredients** together until smooth. Stir dry mixture into wet until smooth.

4. Pour batter into waffle iron and cook for 3-5 minutes until browned evenly and serve.

7. Waffles II

Waffles always taste better when you cover them with fresh maple syrup or fruit sauce. Try making your own strawberry or raspberry syrup to serve over top.

Preparation Time-5 minutes

Servings-4

Ingredients

- 16 ounces all-purpose flour
- 2/3 ounce baking powder
- ¼ teaspoon salt
- 12 ounces milk
- 3 ounces vegetable oil
- 2 separated eggs

Directions

1. Preheat waffle maker and spray surface with a cooking spray.

Preheat waffle iron. Lightly spray with cooking oil.

Whisk baking powder, flour and salt in a big bowl until combined.

Beat milk, egg yolks and vegetable oil in a separate mixing bowl.

In a third bowl, beat the egg whites until you see stiff peaks form.

Stir egg yolk mixture and flour mixture together until smooth and fold in egg whites. Pour in batter and cook for 3-5 minutes until golden brown.

8. Whole Wheat Oat Waffles

This recipe is another for whole wheat waffles that uses oat flour to add a nutty flavour. I like to have these with some sliced banana and sour cream.

Preparation Time-20 minutes

Servings-6

Ingredients

- 4 ounces whole-wheat pastry flour
- 4 ounces all-purpose flour
- 8 ounces oat flour
- 2 ounces white sugar
- ½ ounce baking powder
- ½ teaspoon salt
- 2 separated eggs
- 12 ounces milk
- 1 ounce canola oil
- 1 teaspoon vanilla extract

Directions

1. Preheat your waffle iron and lightly coat with a cooking spray.

2. Whisk all types of flours, white sugar, salt and baking powder in a large mixing bowl until combined.

3. Beat egg yolks, milk, oil and vanilla together in another bowl.

4. In a third bowl, whisk egg whites together until peaks form.

5. Stir milk mixture into dry flour mixture until smooth and fold the egg whites into batter. Let the mixture stand for 5 minutes.

4. Pour batter into waffle iron according to manufacturer's instructions and cook for 2-4 minutes until golden brown.

9. Potato Waffles

These potato waffles make a delicious breakfast or as a side for a light lunch and dinner. Try these with some sour cream and apple sauce for a sweeter flavour.

Preparation Time-20 minutes

Servings-4

Ingredients

- 1 ounce butter
- 1 chopped onion
- ½ ounce garlic, minced
- 16 ounces mashed potatoes
- 2 ounces all-purpose flour
- 2 large eggs
- ¼ teaspoon ground black pepper
- ¼ teaspoon salt

Directions

1. Melt butter in a frying pan on the medium heat and sauté onion and garlic in the butter for 5-7 minutes until tender.

3. Preheat a waffle iron according to the manufacturer instructions.

4. Mix onions with the rest of the **Ingredients** until well combined.

5. Pour batter into waffle iron according to manufacturer's instructions. Cook for 3-5 minutes until golden brown.

10. Mom's Waffles

My mom had a lot of different waffle recipes that she tried over the years. This classic waffle dish was a favourite around my house as a kid.

Preparation Time-5 minutes

Servings-4

Ingredients

- 16 ounces all-purpose flour
- 1/3 ounce baking powder
- 1 ounce white sugar
- 1 teaspoon salt
- 16 ounces milk
- 2 large eggs
- 1 ounce vegetable oil

Directions

1. Preheat your waffle iron and lightly coat with a cooking spray.

2. Whisk flour, sugar, baking powder and salt together in a large mixing bowl.

3. In a separate bowl, beat the eggs, milk and oil together. Stir dry mixture into wet until smooth.

4. Pour batter into the waffle iron and then cook for 3-5 minutes until golden brown. Cook in batches.

11.Chocolate Chip Waffles

Who doesn't love chocolate chips in waffles? This recipe tastes more like a dessert than a breakfast and I have served after a meal before with some ice cream.

Preparation Time-15 minutes

Servings-10

Ingredients

- 12 ounces all-purpose flour
- 2 ½ ounces powdered buttermilk
- ¼ ounce baking powder
- ½ teaspoon baking soda
- 8 ounces milk
- 2 ounces heavy cream
- 2 egg yolks
- 2 ounces melted butter
- 2 egg whites
- 8 ounces mini chocolate chips, semisweet

Directions

1. Preheat your waffle iron and coat surface lightly with a cooking spray.

2. Mix flour, buttermilk powder, baking powder and soda in a large mixing bowl.

3. Beat cream with an electric mixer. Beat in milk, yolks and butter until smooth.

4. Stir wet mixture into dry flour mixture until smooth.

5. Beat egg whites in a separate bowl until gentle peaks form.

6. Fold egg whites and chocolate into the batter and pour into the waffle iron.

7. Cook for 3-5 minutes until golden brown.

12.Cornmeal Waffles

When you are looking for waffles with less flour, try these cornmeal waffles for your next meal. I like to eat them with some bananas and yogurt.

Preparation Time-20 minutes

Servings-12

Ingredients

- 8 ounces whole wheat flour
- 12 ounces cornmeal
- 1 ¼ ounces white sugar
- 1 ounce baking powder
- 4 egg whites
- ¾ teaspoon baking soda
- 14 ounces nonfat buttermilk

Directions

Preheat a waffle iron, and then coat with a cooking spray.

Whisk flour, cornmeal, sugar, baking powder and soda together in a large mixing bowl until combined.

Make a well in the middle of the flour mixture and stir in buttermilk until just combined and smooth.

Whip egg whites in another bowl until peaks form and fold egg whites into batter.

Pour batter into the waffle iron according to manufacturer's instructions and cook for 3-5 minutes until golden brown.

13. Buttermilk Prairie Waffles

These buttermilk treats are creamy and rich when served with some melted butter and whipped cream. I like to have some applesauce and berries on the table when I serve them.

Preparation Time-15 minutes

Servings-8

Ingredients

- 16 ounces flour, sifted
- 1 teaspoon baking soda
- 1 teaspoon baking powder
- 1 teaspoon salt
- 4 room temperature eggs
- 16 ounces buttermilk
- 8 ounces butter, melted

Directions

Preheat your waffle iron and coat surface lightly with a cooking spray.

Whisk flour, soda, baking powder and salt in a large mixing bowl until combined.

Beat eggs in a separate bowl and stir into flour mixture until smooth.

Stir in the butter and pour the batter into waffle iron. Cook for 3-5 minutes until golden brown.

14. Chocolate Waffles I

This waffle recipe is another made for breakfast or a sweet treat after a meal. I like to serve it with some chocolate sauce and ice cream.

Preparation Time-5 minutes

Servings-10

Ingredients

- 12 ounces all-purpose flour
- ½ teaspoon salt
- 3 teaspoons baking powder
- 4 ounces white sugar
- 1 ½ ounces cocoa powder, unsweetened
- 8 ounces milk
- 2 large eggs
- 2 ounces melted butter
- ½ ounce softened butter
- 6 ounces confectioners' sugar
- 1 teaspoon milk
- ½ teaspoon vanilla extract

Directions

1. Preheat waffle iron. Coat surface lightly with a cooking spray.

2. Whisk flour, salt, baking powder, cocoa and sugar together in a large mixing bowl until combined.

3. In another bowl, beat milk, eggs and butter together. Stir wet mixture into dry until smooth.

4. For sauce - stir butter, confectioners' sugar, vanilla and milk in a separate bowl until stiffened.

5. Pour waffle batter into waffle iron for 3-5 minutes until golden brown and serve with sauce.

15. Puff Pastry Waffles

These light and airy waffles make a lovely brunch treat when you are entertaining. I like to have some whipped cream and fresh strawberries on the side.

Preparation Time-5 minutes

Servings-8

Ingredients

- 17 ¼ ounce thawed package frozen puff pastry
- Pam cooking spray

Directions

1. Preheat your waffle iron and lightly coat with a cooking spray.

2. Line a hard surface with parchment and roll puff pastry out.

3. Cut each sheet of pastry into 4 squares.

4. Place one square in the waffle iron and cook for 3-5 minutes until golden brown.

5. Repeat process until puff pastry is all cooked.

16. Wonderful Waffles

These waffles are wonderful when served with some sour cream and bananas. Try this recipe for lunch or dinner when you want a treat.

Preparation Time-15 minutes

Servings-6

Ingredients

- 1 teaspoon baking powder
- ½ teaspoon salt
- 2 ounces butter
- 18 ounces all-purpose flour
- 2 ounces brown sugar
- 3 large separated eggs
- 1 teaspoon baking soda
- 16 ounces buttermilk

Directions

1. Preheat your waffle iron and coat in cooking spray

2. Whisk flour, soda, baking powder and salt in a large mixing bowl until combined.

3. Cream butter and sugar until fluffy. Beat in egg yolks.

4. Stir in flour mixture and buttermilk alternately into batter.

5. Beat egg whites in a large glass bowl until stiff peaks form.

6. Fold in a third of the egg whites to the batter followed by the other two thirds.

7. Pour the batter into the waffle iron and then cook for 3-5 minutes until golden brown.

17. Pumpkin Waffles

I like to make these waffles in the Fall when pumpkins are in season. Try this recipe with some whipped cream and applesauce.

Preparation Time-30 minutes

Servings-6

Ingredients

- 20 ounces all-purpose flour
- 1/3 ounce baking powder
- 1/3 ounce cinnamon, ground
- 1 teaspoon allspice, ground
- 1 teaspoon ginger, ground
- ½ teaspoon salt
- 2 ounces brown sugar, packed
- 8 ounces canned pumpkin
- 16 ounces milk
- 4 separated eggs
- 2 ounces melted butter

Apple Cider Syrup

- 4 ounces white sugar
- ½ ounce cornstarch
- 1 teaspoon cinnamon, ground
- 8 ounces apple cider
- ½ ounce lemon juice
- 1 ounce butter

Directions

1. Preheat your waffle iron and lightly coat with a cooking spray.

2. Whisk flour, cinnamon, baking powder, ginger, allspice, salt and brown sugar in a large mixing bowl until combined.

3. In a separate mixing bowl, mix pumpkin, egg yolks and milk together

4. Whip egg whites in a glass bowl until peaks form.

5. Stir flour mixture and 2 ounces of melted butter into the pumpkin mix until well combined.

6. Fold in 1/3 of the egg whites to the mixture followed by the remaining egg whites.

7. Spoon the batter into the waffle iron according to manufacturer's instructions and cook for 3-5 minutes until golden brown.

8. In a medium saucepan, combine all ingredients except for butter on medium heat until just at a boil.

9.Remove syrup from heat and stir in 1 ounce of butter. Serve with waffles.

18. Belgian Waffles

Who hasn't thought of Belgian waffles when the word 'waffle" is mentioned? I love to serve these with some fresh fruit and yogurt.

Preparation Time-10 minutes

Servings-6

Ingredients

- 2 eggs, separated
- 2 ½ ounces white sugar
- ¼ ounce vanilla extract
- 4 ounces melted butter
- 1 teaspoon salt
- 22 ounces self-rising flour
- 16 ounces warm milk

Directions

1. Preheat your waffle iron and lightly coat with a cooking spray.

2. Beat egg yolks and sugar in a large mixing bowl and beat in vanilla. Beat in butter and salt until smooth.

3. Mix flour and milk alternately until well blended.

4. Beat egg whites in a mixing bowl until peaks form.

5. Fold egg whites into batter and let it sit for 45 minutes.

6. Ladle batter into waffle iron and cook until golden brown.

19. Deluxe Waffles

These deluxe waffles can be served as breakfast or brunch food, when served with some yogurt. I also like to serve them with fresh raspberries, strawberries and whipped cream.

Preparation Time-10 minutes

Servings-6

Ingredients

- 16 ounces all-purpose flour
- ½ ounce baking powder
- 1 teaspoon salt
- 1 ½ ounces white sugar
- 4 eggs, separated
- 10 ounces milk
- 4 ounces vegetable oil

Directions

1. Whisk flour, baking powder, white sugar and salt in a large mixing bowl until combined.

2. Beat egg yolks, milk and oil together in a separate mixing bowl. Make a well in the center of the dry mixture and pour egg yolk mixture into the well. Stir until just moistened.

3. Beat egg whites until peaks form and fold into the batter. Spoon batter into waffle iron and cook for 3-5 minutes until golden brown.

20. Easy Waffles

These waffles have a lovely tangy flavour when you add lemon zest. I like to serve these with some orange slices and whipped cream.

Preparation Time-10 minutes

Servings-4

Ingredients

- 16 ounces all-purpose flour
- 1/3 ounce baking powder
- 1 ounce white sugar
- ½ teaspoon salt
- 2 eggs, separated
- 1 ounce lemon zest, grated
- 1 teaspoon vanilla extract
- 16 ounces milk
- 3 ounces melted butter

Directions

1. Preheat your waffle iron and coat surface in cooking spray

2. Stir flour, sugar, baking powder and salt in a large bowl

3. In another bowl, beat the egg whites until stiff peaks form.

4. In third bowl, whisk lemon zest, vanilla extract and egg yolks until smooth. Whisk butter into wet **Ingredients** followed by egg whites.

5. Pour wet **Ingredients** into dry until smooth

6. Ladle the batter into the waffle iron and then cook for 3-5 minutes until golden brown

21. Banana Waffles

Try these banana waffles with yogurt or sour cream. Chocolate sauce also makes a delicious side with ice cream when serving them for dessert.

Preparation Time-10 minutes

Servings-4

Ingredients

- 10 ounces all-purpose flour
- ½ ounce baking powder
- ½ teaspoon salt
- a pinch nutmeg, ground
- 8 ounces skim milk
- 1 large egg

2 sliced ripened bananas

Directions

1. Preheat waffle maker and coat surface with a cooking spray.

2. Whisk flour, baking powder, nutmeg and salt in a large bowl until combined.

3. Add milk and egg to the dry ingredients until smooth.

4. Spoon 1 ounce of batter onto the waffle iron and place banana slices on top. Cook for 3-5 minutes until golden brown

22. Norwegian Waffles

Norway knows how to make a delicious waffle and now so do you! This Norwegian waffle recipe I simple and delicious when served with some yogurt.

Preparation Time-10 minutes

Servings-4

Ingredients

- 2 large eggs
- 1 ounce white sugar
- 1 ½ ounces shortening, melted
- 14 ounces milk
- 1 teaspoon vanilla extract
- 1 teaspoon salt
- 12 ounces all-purpose flour
- 3 ½ teaspoons baking powder

Directions

1. Preheat a waffle iron and coat surface with a cooking spray.

2. Beat eggs and white sugar together until light and fluffy.

3. Add melted shortening, milk, vanilla extract and salt to the egg mixture and stir until blended.

4. Whisk flour and baking powder together in a separate bowl and add to the wet ingredients. Stir until smooth.

5. Pour 5 ½ ounces of batter into the waffle iron and cook for 3-5 minutes until golden brown.

23. Yeast Waffles

Try these waffles with active dry yeast for a change in flavour and texture. I like to serve these with some butter and applesauce.

Preparation Time-10 minutes

Servings-6

Ingredients

- 16 ounces milk
- ¼ ounce package active dry yeast
- 4 ounces warm water
- 4 ounces melted butter
- 1 teaspoon white sugar
- 1 teaspoon salt
- 24 ounces unbleached all-purpose flour, sifted
- 2 slightly beaten eggs
- ½ teaspoon baking soda

Directions

1. Heat milk in a pan until it starts bubbling. Remove pan from heat.

2. Pour warm water into a measuring cup and dissolve yeast in the water. Leave for 10 minutes.

3. Mix warm milk, dissolved yeast, salt, butter, sugar and all-purpose flour in a large bowl until smooth.

4. Cover the bowl and leave mixture at room temperature overnight

5. Stir eggs and baking soda into yeast mixture until well combined.

6. Spoon batter in the waffle iron and cook for 3-5 minutes until golden brown

24. Blueberries Waffles

I like to serve these waffles with fresh blueberries and sour cream for breakfast. I use organic, raw honey for the **Ingredients** for a fresher flavour.

Preparation Time-20 minutes

Servings-6

Ingredients

- 3 eggs, separated into yolks and whites and beaten
- 13 ½ ounces milk
- 16 ounces all-purpose flour
- 2 ¼ teaspoons baking powder
- ½ teaspoon salt
- 2 ounces butter, melted
- 5 ½ ounces blueberries
- 12 ounces blueberries
- 1 ½ ounces honey
- 4 ounces orange juice
- ½ ounce cornstarch

Directions

1. Preheat your waffle iron and coat surface with a cooking spray.

2. Beat egg yolks and milk together in a large mixing bowl. Add flour, baking powder and salt into the egg yolks mixture until smooth.

3. Add butter to the mixture and stir well. Let mixture sit for 30 minutes.

4. Fold egg whites into the batter and fold 5 ½ ounces of blueberries in as well.

5. Pour batter into the waffle iron and cook for 3-5 minutes until golden brown.

5. For the sauce, mix 12 ounces of blueberries, 2 ounces of orange juice and honey in a medium pan on medium heat and bring to a boil.

6. In a separate bowl, combine the rest of the orange juice and cornstarch. Add cornstarch mixture to the blueberries in the pan and stir well until thickened. Serve sauce with waffles.

25. Cinnamon Pumpkin Waffles

These waffles taste and smell amazing when you whip up a batch for a morning treat. I like to serve these with some whipped cream and apple slices.

Preparation Time-10 minutes

Servings-4

Ingredients

- 8 ounces whole wheat flour
- 2 ounces wheat germ
- 2 ½ ounces white sugar
- 1 teaspoon cinnamon, ground
- ½ teaspoon nutmeg, ground
- 1 teaspoon pumpkin pie spice
- ½ teaspoon salt
- ½ ounce baking powder
- 6 ounces milk
- 4 ounces pumpkin puree
- 1 ounce melted butter
- 1 ounce olive oil
- 4 ounces unsweetened applesauce
- 1 large egg
- 1 large egg white
- 4 ounces pecans, chopped

Directions

1. Preheat waffle maker and spray surface with a cooking spray.

2. Whisk flour, sugar, wheat germ, pumpkin spice, cinnamon, nutmeg, baking powder and salt until well combined.

3. Beat milk, puree, oil, butter, applesauce, egg and egg white in another bowl until smooth.

4. Stir dry mixture into the pumpkin puree mixture. Fold pecans into the batter.

5. Ladle batter into the waffle iron and cook for 3-5 minutes until golden brown.

26. Almond Flour Waffles

Almond flour is a great substitute for all-purpose flour when you are on Keto. I like to serve these with some shaved dark chocolate and fresh raspberries.

Preparation Time-10 minutes

Servings-6

Ingredients

- 8 ounces almond flour
- a pinch salt
- 1 teaspoon baking soda
- 4 large eggs
- 1 teaspoon vanilla extract
- 2 ounces honey
- cooking spray

Directions

1. Preheat your waffle iron and coat surface with a cooking spray..

2. Whisk flour, soda and salt in a mixing bowl until well combined.

3. Beat eggs, honey and vanilla extract together. Stir dry mixture into wet mixture until smooth.

4. Spoon batter into waffle maker and cook for 3-5 minutes until golden brown.

27. Yogurt Waffles

The yogurt in these waffles make them creamy and delicious. I like to serve these with some whipped cream and sliced fresh strawberries.

Preparation Time-10 minutes

Servings-4

Ingredients

- 3 large eggs
- 12 ounces vanilla yogurt, fat-free
- 10 ounces all-purpose flour
- 1/3 ounce baking powder
- ½ teaspoon kosher salt
- 1 teaspoon baking soda
- 4 ounces shortening

Directions

1. Preheat your waffle iron and coat surface with a cooking spray.

2. In a large bowl, beat eggs and yogurt together. Add flour, baking powder, soda, salt and shortening to the mixture and mix until smooth.

3. Spoon batter into a waffle iron and cook for 3-5 minutes until golden brown.

28. Gingerbread Waffles with Hot Chocolate

This waffle recipe is perfect for breakfast on a cold winter morning. The flavour of chocolate and gingerbread smell heavenly and put me in the mood for the holidays.

Preparation Time-25 minutes

Servings-6

Ingredients

- 8 ounces light molasses
- 4 ounces butter
- ¼ ounce baking soda
- 4 ounces milk
- 1 large egg
- 16 ounces all-purpose flour
- ¼ ounce ground ginger
- ½ teaspoon cinnamon, ground
- ½ teaspoon salt
- 16 ounces boiling water
- 8 ounces white sugar
- 1 ounce cornstarch
- 4 ounces cocoa powder, unsweetened
- 1/3 ounce vanilla extract
- 1 teaspoon salt
- 1 ounce butter

Directions

Preheat your waffle iron and coat surface with a cooking spray.

Heat molasses and 2 ounces of butter in a small pan and bring to a simmer. Remove pan from heat and cool for 2 minutes.

Stir in milk, egg and soda.

Whisk flour, cinnamon, ginger and salt together in a large mixing bowl. Make a well in the middle of the flour mixture and stir in molasses mixture until smooth.

Spoon batter onto the waffle iron and cook for 3-5 minutes until golden brown.

For sauce - heat water, 8 ounces of white sugar, cocoa powder, cornstarch and 1

teaspoon of salt in a saucepan on medium heat.

Stir continuously until the mixture comes to a boil. Remove the pan from the heat and then stir in vanilla and 1 ounce of butter until smooth and thickened. Serve sauce with waffles.

29. Beer Batter Waffles

These waffles make a great snack for watching the game or for a holiday weekend. I like to serve these with some butter and whipped cream.

Preparation Time-15 minutes

Servings-6

Ingredients

- 16 ounces self-rising flour
- 12 ounces beer
- 4 ounces melted butter, unsalted
- 2 ounces milk
- 2 eggs, separated
- ½ ounce honey
- 1 teaspoon vanilla extract

Directions

Preheat waffle maker and coat surface with a cooking spray.

Mix all the ingredients in a big bowl and stir until smooth.

Beat egg whites in a separate bowl until stiff peaks form.

Spoon the batter into the waffle iron and cook for 3-5 minutes until golden brown.

30. Vegan Waffles

The vegans in your home will love these waffles when you serve them for breakfast. I like to serve these with fresh fruit and a bit of vegan ice cream.

Preparation Time-15 minutes

Servings-6

Ingredients

- 3 ounces water
- 1 ounce flax seed meal
- 8 ounces rolled oats
- 14 ounces soy milk
- 4 ounces whole wheat flour
- 4 ounces all-purpose flour
- 1 ounce canola oil
- 2/3 ounce baking powder
- 1 teaspoon vanilla extract
- ½ teaspoon salt
- ½ ounce agave nectar

Directions

Preheat a waffle iron and coat the surface with a cooking spray.

2. Mix water and flax seed in a small bowl together

3. Place oats in a food processor and blend into a flour. Add the rest of the ingredients to the food processor and blend until combined.

4. Spoon 4 ounces into a waffle iron and cook for 3-5 minutes until golden brown.

Conclusion

From classic to vegan, the waffle recipes in this cookbook are delicious and filling. There is a dish for every taste so you can serve a different type of waffle every day of the month if you want and never get bored. When breakfast is calling, or any other meal of the day, a waffle is always sure to please.

About the Author

A native of Albuquerque, New Mexico, Sophia Freeman found her calling in the culinary arts when she enrolled at the Sante Fe School of Cooking. Freeman decided to take a year after graduation and travel around Europe, sampling the cuisine from small bistros and family owned restaurants from Italy to Portugal. Her bubbly personality and inquisitive nature made her popular with the locals in the villages and when she finished her trip and came home, she had made friends for life in the places she had visited. She also came home with a deeper understanding of European cuisine.

Freeman went to work at one of Albuquerque's 5-star restaurants as a sous-chef and soon worked her way up to head chef. The restaurant began to feature Freeman's original dishes as specials on the menu and soon after, she began to write e-books with her recipes. Sophia's dishes mix local flavours with European inspiration making them irresistible to the diners in her restaurant and the online community.

Freeman's experience in Europe didn't just teach her new ways of cooking, but also unique methods of presentation. Using rich sauces, crisp vegetables and meat cooked to perfection, she creates a stunning display as well as a delectable dish. She has won many local awards for her cuisine and she continues to delight her diners with her culinary masterpieces.

Author's Afterthoughts

I want to convey my big thanks to all of my readers who have taken the time to read my book. Readers like you make my work so rewarding and I cherish each and every one of you.

Grateful cannot describe how I feel when I know that someone has chosen my work over all of the choices available online. I hope you enjoyed the book as much as I enjoyed writing it.

Feedback from my readers is how I grow and learn as a chef and an author. Please take the time to let me know your thoughts by leaving a review on Amazon so I and your fellow readers can learn from your experience.

My deepest thanks,

Sophia Freeman

Printed in Great Britain
by Amazon